This edition published in 1992 by Rainbow Books,
Elsley House, 24–30 Great Titchfield Street, London W1P 7AD

Originally published in 1989 as *Animal Life Stories: The Hedgehog* by
Kingfisher Books.

ISBN 1 871745 68 3

Black and white illustrations by Jean Colville.
End papers by Maurice Pledger.

Printed and bound in Spain.

EYE-VIEW LIBRARY

THE
HEDGEHOG

By Angela Royston

Illustrated by Maurice Pledger

RAINBOW
·BOOKS·

All winter the hedgehog has slept, safe in her underground nest. Now the weather is warmer and she wakes up to see if spring has really come.

As she pushes up through the soil she smells the flowers and new leaves. She hears a mouse rustling, doves cooing and pheasants pecking in the grass.

The hedgehog is weak and hungry after her long winter sleep. When it gets dark she snuffles around and eats a slug. Then she finds a newt. Quickly she presses her spines into it and bites its tasty flesh.

All night the hedgehog searches the wood for food.
She listens out for foxes and badgers who might
attack her. By morning she is no longer hungry and
falls asleep, safely hidden under a pile of leaves.

One night, a week or two later, the hedgehog hears a male hedgehog scuffling along behind her. She hisses at him to make him go away, but he just hisses back.

Snorting and grunting he runs around her for
nearly three hours, slowly getting closer and closer.
At last she is no longer scared of him and lets him
mate with her.

The male hedgehog goes off to look for food and finds a skylark's nest. The skylark cannot stop him smashing her eggs and sucking up their yolks. But a hungry fox is watching nearby. The hedgehog smells the fox and knows he has little chance of escape. Terrified, he rolls up into a prickly ball, to try and protect himself.

The fox hits the hedgehog with her paw and he rolls downhill and splashes into a stream. He quickly unrolls so that he can swim, and the fast stream carries him out of the fox's reach. He has been lucky this time.

A litter of baby hedgehogs are growing inside the female, and after a month she looks for a safe place to have her babies. She finds a hole at the bottom of a stone wall and fills it with a soft bed of leaves.

The newborn babies feed all the time on their
mother's milk. Soft white spines grow on their
backs, but soon they are replaced by hundreds of
hard brown ones.

When the young hedgehogs are about a month old
their mother takes them hunting with her, mainly
for insects and worms. But one night they find a
poisonous snake.

The mother rushes around it, then charges as the snake strikes with its poisonous fangs. The snake is trapped on the hedgehog's sharp spines and it cannot escape.

After their exciting meal the tired young hedgehogs return to their nest. But a hungry fox is passing by and he smells them. As he pushes his nose into the nest the mother hedgehog snorts at him bravely. The hole is too small for the fox. Although he pushes hard he cannot get in and has to go away hungry.

That night the mother hedgehog and her family
scuttle silently through the wood. Luckily they do
not meet the fox and soon they find a tree with huge
old roots. They make a new, safer nest under the
roots, where the fox will not find them.

Summer has come and the young hedgehogs are
growing fast. They spend more and more time
hunting on their own. One by one they are able to
leave the nest and their mother for good, and find
nests of their own.

Soon the summer is over. As the days grow colder, the hedgehog hunts busily by day and by night, eating whatever she can. She needs to be well fed and fat to see her through the long cold winter.

When winter comes the hedgehog creeps under a big, thick fungus and covers herself with a layer of soil and dry leaves. Here she will stay warm and safe until spring.

More About Hedgehogs

The hedgehog in this story lives only in Europe. It has short legs and a fat body and is about as big as a loaf of bread. Other kinds of hedgehog live in Africa and Asia.

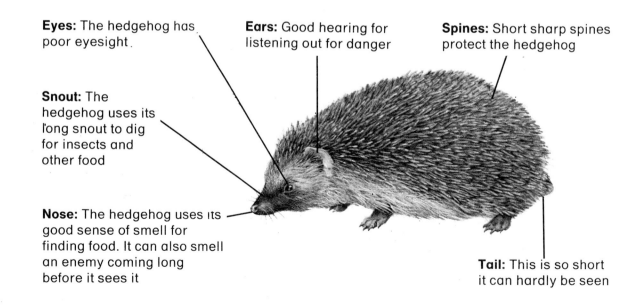

Eyes: The hedgehog has poor eyesight.

Ears: Good hearing for listening out for danger

Spines: Short sharp spines protect the hedgehog

Snout: The hedgehog uses its long snout to dig for insects and other food

Nose: The hedgehog uses its good sense of smell for finding food. It can also smell an enemy coming long before it sees it

Tail: This is so short it can hardly be seen

Hedgehogs hibernate when the weather gets very cold. Hibernation is not really the same as sleeping, although it seems a bit like it. The hedgehog curls up in its nest and shuts its eyes. Its body becomes cooler, but not as cold as the snow outside. It uses little energy and eats no food until the weather warms up and it begins to stir again.

The hedgehogs in the picture above are rolling on fallen apples and carrying them on their spines to their nest. This picture is very old, and no one knows whether hedgehogs really do this.